T0083841

The Selected Poems of Max Jacob

The
SELECTED POEMS
of
MAX JACOB

edited and translated by
William Kulik

Oberlin College Press

www.oberlin.edu/~ocpress

Publication of this book was supported in part by a
grant from the Ohio Arts Council.

Ohio Arts Council
A STATE AGENCY
THAT SUPPORTS PUBLIC
PROGRAMS IN THE ARTS

Library of Congress Cataloging-in-Publication Data

Jacob, Max (translations and introduction by William
Kulik)
        The Selected Poems of Max Jacob
        (The FIELD Translation Series v. 24)
        I. Title.   II. Series.

LC: 99-068954
ISBN: 0-932440-86-X (pbk.)

to Stephen Berg

Contents

Introduction
by William Kulik

Friday, August 12, 1916, a sunny day in the middle of the war. Jean Cocteau has his mother's camera, taking an afternoon's worth of photos of "the Picasso gang" hanging out at the Rotonde, hamming it up on the boulevards of Montparnasse. With Pablo and his latest mistress are the painters Ortiz de Zarate, Moise Kisling and Modigliani, poets André Salmon and Max Jacob. Max, always the dandy in fitted suit, bowler, monocle and walking stick. Max the irrepressible, brilliant conversationalist, his greatest work, *Le cornet á dès (The Dice Cup)*, hidden in a trunk because he isn't sure it's any good. Max the hypersensitive, masking his anguish behind what many called compulsive clowning. Student of astrology and numerology, believer in the Kabbala, Jew turned Christian after his 1909 vision of Christ on the wall of his room, only baptized ("Cyprien") six years later as one priest after the other doubted that the revelation of this strange man was authentic. Picasso believed, in it and in him, but even though he stood for him and Max invariably began his letters to the painter with "Dear Godfather," their long, intimate, intensely productive relationship was by this time frayed, mostly because of Picasso's wealth and fame—and Max's lack of either.

From their first meeting, in 1901, when Max, then an art critic, enthused over the unknown painter's work, the two became close friends: the little Jew from

Quimper in Celtic Brittany, land of churches and pardons, who had come to Paris to study painting, and the little Spaniard with colossal talent and an ego to match, who, though he knew next to no French, listened to Max read the poems he'd secretly been writing, and called him France's greatest poet. The sad fact is that Max, "poor clown," believed him, insisting that if it hadn't been for Picasso, he'd never have become a writer. Later, when Max was deep in poverty and despair, sick of the menial, humiliating jobs that drained his creative energies, Picasso told him to shave, replace his pince-nez with a monocle, and just write. As always, he felt Pablo's power was irresistible, and confessed to feeling like a courtesan who imitates her sovereign, seeing himself "the poor little Jew who doesn't think he's a poet" with his "terrible and charming prince." Yet in their shared poverty and dedication to art, they would never be closer.

Fernande Olivier, Picasso's mistress—and therefore Max's rival—recalls the Mondays when Max received guests at his hovel a few doors away from Picasso's studio, describing the mood as "conspiratorial." "And why not?" she asks, "Weren't we conspiring against everything established in matters of art?" The man who was to become the great animator of that spirit of revolt, Guillaume Apollinaire, came on the Montmartre scene in 1905. Brilliant, ebullient, a clever organizer and promoter, he became Picasso's first publicist and Max's first publisher. Soon they were three together, one for all and all for art, the core of an avant-garde that in time swelled to include Braque, Juan Gris, Modigliani, Satie, Cocteau, André Salmon,

Pierre Reverdy and André Derain. As Roger Shattuck says in his landmark study of the era, *The Banquet Years*: "to a greater extent than at any time since the Renaissance, painters, writers and musicians lived and worked together in an atmosphere of perpetual collaboration."[1]

But not always. Competition often ruled: between Picasso and Braque, between Jacob and Apollinaire. Effeminate Max wounded much too easily, and aggressive Apollinaire often enjoyed wounding him— as did macho Pablo. Still, their camaraderie was sustained by a commitment to what Apollinaire called "the New Spirit" of modernism in the arts. For their part, Max and Guillaume despised the sloppy romanticism and self-pity they associated with Symbolist poetry as much as their painter friends hated the bourgeois realism of salon art. "Down with Laforgue!" they'd shout, careening along the narrow, winding cobblestone streets, back from parties where Guillaume declaimed and Max entertained.

Both had books published by the astute and enterprising art dealer, Daniel-Henry Kahnweiler, who conceived the idea of matching artists in his stable with innovative writers. Apollinaire's book was illustrated by Derain, Jacob's by Picasso—his first illustrations for a text. And it was Kahnweiler who, in 1907, hearing of the weird painting later known as *Les Demoiselles d'Avignon*, visited Picasso's studio and was both thunderstruck by, and at the same time uniquely

---

[1]Doubleday (New York, 1961), 29.

appreciative of, what Picasso was attempting: a revolution in visual art, a new way of seeing based less on a representation of reality than on a rendering of its essence in an attempt to create a three-dimensional structure on a flat surface—at least in the figures on the right half, with their misplaced body parts and distorted features. There, Kahnweiler was later to say, Cubism originated.

Jacob once wrote a semi-comic piece called "Thirteen Reasons Why I Didn't Create Cubism" (among them: "Because hearing only that spoken of I got great pleasure out of thinking of something else" and "Because Picasso chose Braque as his pupil, not me"). He also said, much later, that he'd been "writing Cubist" since 1903, though his groundbreaking work, *Le cornet à dés*, wasn't published until 1917. The book, a collection of pieces ranging from a single paragraph to a page and a half long, immediately established Max as the "renewer" of the prose poem.

These little "objects" have a clarity and resonance resulting from the careful placement of images that have been "worked," as Picasso said a Cubist canvas must be—"only by allusion to reality." In the preface to the book, Max speaks of "transplanting" elements from reality and "situating" them in novel relationships to one another by unforeseeable juxtapositions—rarely as they would be found in quotidian, five-senses reality, but as they might instead be experienced in dream or in fantasy. They are never, as Cocteau said of them, "the result of what its *subject* determines but the *actions*, the *designs* evoked by [Jacob's] imagination." Max said he "never felt more Cubist" than when he arrived at the autonomous, self-contained reality of this new prose poem "by means of the unreal"—reality "bent" to suit his needs.[2]

But why present the reader with the challenges of such an unpredictable universe? Mainly to frustrate his expectations for a story that would confirm *his* reality by reflecting it—Max abhorred any art "which has value only by comparison with the real." Instead, he wanted to shake the reader out of his complacency, open his eyes, through comic irony, to "the absurdity of our rituals and the things we hold dear." So he sets him up by appearing to give him what he's looking for; then—often no more than an image or a sentence later—knocks him down, thus inducing, by means of this assemblage, "the little shock of doubt" he considered the primary aesthetic emotion that creates the distance—"the margin of silence"—between the poem itself and the reader's expectations. It makes sense that one of his favorite means of keeping a reader off balance is parody: the send-up of familiar genres. In these, clichés of content and style are exposed by exaggerating them to the point of absurdity, creating what might be called pseudo- or anti-genre genres. As in

---

[2]Art as an expression of will was essential to Jacob—"the will to exteriorize oneself by chosen means." In a 1936 letter, Max elaborated on that definition using the image of one ellipse inside another: "I'm in the middle (Max Jacob), I have my subject, which circles the ellipse, at first near me, then further . . . and further . . . it almost disappears but I observe it, as it comes back to me. I am always at the center: *it is necessary to direct and not to be directed* . . . to attract the reader and sometimes lose him one can make the subject 'leap' to a 2nd ellipse and reverse direction."

"Biographical," for instance, with its inane play on the "remarkable" talent of its subject and how "regrettable" it was that the talent had not been "remarked"; or "A Bit of Art Criticism," where ridiculous reasons are given for the origins of the painter's style. There are also parodies of memoir, journalism, the novel, the fairy tale and—with special vengeance—poetry and literature with a capital L ("Literature and Poetry," and "Literary Standards"). A pseudo (auto-)-biographical "I" is also responsible for some deft play on received ideas concerning the boundaries between Art and Reality: notably in the poem (titled "Poem") that begins with the desire to "erase the heads of the generals of the Empire" as if they were in a drawing, acknowledges the impossibility (because they're real), then pictures Max Jacob and Miss Leonie walking around in one of the illustrations for Max's novel, *Saint Matorel*. Pseudo-Max even says he knows the engraver. The "elements" are all real: "Miss Leonie" was Max's only heterosexual lover, the novel and its author exist in fact. And of course he knows the engraver: it was Picasso. The critical question is raised when Max, speaking logically, says, "The generals of the Empire are alive; doesn't that mean that Miss Leonie and I are, too?" The whole issue achieves a high level of unresolvability—the result of Max's sweet irony—when he re-enters the woodcut and "peace reigned in the desert of art."

Even where parody is not the object, there is always a comic toying with reality, a constant reminder that what you're reading is a poem, a thing that, he insists, obeys the laws of the poet's mind. In "Allusion to a Circus Act," you are first told there are birds in the sky, then immediately told "there is no sky." Playing with the reader's sense of reality is not all he does. Sometimes the poet's pseudo-biographical mask slips a bit to reveal real feeling (unless it's pseudo-"real feeling"): "Sad Last Appeal to the Phantoms Inspirations from the Past" seems legitimately nostalgic, while in "The Concarneau Regatta" a delicate irony balances self-pity and self-mockery the way it does in the best of Jewish humor.

And there is something else, something reaching for the core of psychic truth: poems in which the "margin of silence" seems meant to elicit wonder and make us question facile assumptions about motive. "Errors of Mercy," especially, where crime and punishment may be the issue, and "Let's Bring Back the Old Themes," a savage joke, an artist's take on what people *really* feel about culture that goes largely unspoken—except for Goering, that true primitive, who said, "When I hear culture spoken of, I draw my revolver."

To a greater degree than most of his contemporaries, Max believed in the need to tap the raw psychic energy of the unconscious, which he called "the only genuine article." He loved the stories of Kafka ("the Dostoevsky of Surrealism") because he felt they embodied that energy. He spent fifteen years studying dreams until he was so familiar with their peculiar language he could invent them. Many of his poems—in prose and in verse—*were*, in fact, either invented dreams, their inspiration a dream image, or a fantasy, a pun, a slip of the tongue, eye or pen, all of which he felt, with Freud, were signals from a buried world that we could continue to deny only at our peril. His primary goal became, like that of the Surrealists, to "make the unconscious conscious," or, as Tzara said, "to unite dream and action," by giving the language of the unconscious free expression.

But just as Max was no Literary Man, he was no Surrealist either. He claimed the movement stole from him, perverting his original goal, and he mocked its efforts at the direct transmission of the unconscious via sleep-speech and automatic writing as simple-minded and "subjectivist." Rather than simply record a stream of raw data, he tried to replicate the feel of a dream, its eerie calm, its incredible but matter-of-fact metamorphoses in the apparently random sequences of his poems, which seem arbitrary but are based on the association of ideas. And, just as Max trusted that images which succeed each other in dreams are related by an internal logic that defies rational analysis, he also believed in the power of free-association to lure and tame that fabulous beast, the poem.

He was adamant that "a poet must be mad for words, completely absorbed by them, intoxicated, the way a painter is with color or form." He read the Larousse daily, discovering "so many words we don't know or we forget." When he found one especially intriguing he'd "bend it, turn it, turn it back," until it had for him "the germ of an idea." Then, as he meditated on it, the word "began a descent" inside him, picking up additional words—"an increasing flow of sparks"— from his rapid-fire associations to them; the words forming phrases, then lines, even stanzas, until only at last (maybe not even then) an understanding of the poem. What the poem "meant" in rational terms was less important to him than what it meant on the level of feeling. "We must," he says, "experience emotionally what the words are telling us, even if we don't understand [them]. There are other ways to understand."

Which may explain how we need to read some of the poems in his second collection, *Le laboratoire central (The Central Laboratory)*. "To Mr. Modigliani To Prove I'm a Poet" tells us that as a child Max felt he was inspired by angels. Now divinely-inspired madness, the *furor poeticus*, is one thing, but a far cry from what Max the adult said about life "down here": "Everything is a play on words." So we should expect punning, commonplaces out of context, often in combination with words "chosen" primarily for their sound. In these poems, the "flow of sparks" generates a lot of heat and a special light which needs to be accepted for what it is: bright, colorful, shifting. Best read as a voyage, crazed and wonderful, to a strange and zany land. Max, with "comic-opera" in his belly, free-associates word to word, phrase to phrase, whipping up such froth as "Leon! Leon!" ("I'll drive a nail into your hand, armchair arm . . . nails into your board feet") or "Absurd Metamorphosis," which is just that, a series of nutty changes ("A pilot in a suitcase/ All bottled up in the big flask") ending you couldn't guess where. In that sense, not so different from many of the poems in *The Dice Cup*, but feeling so, as if the poet is content to let loose a bit. Bravura efforts, fun to read.

Sometimes there's even more going on: the poem that begins "To hurl a wing at that pearl, a helmet" gives you a view, behind the tumble of images, of the poet himself. "The Tough Guy's Lament," Tzara's favorite for its "subtle irony," also shows the poet whose desires "keep me here/ With demons and daughters of the street," a mild expression of the profane side of Max.

There is a sacred side, too. A little poem from the mid-twenties, "The Chromosome," depicts a world "polarized" by "two deities at either end," one pleasurable but disgusting, the other "a delight" that fills the heart with love. "Every human being," he says, "is drawn to one or the other to the extent that he contains elements of one or the other." That Max experienced both, profoundly, is clear from the poetry. Typical of the profane side are poems such as "Festival" and "Malachites" (with its hint of orgy). The strange "Glass of Blood" that imagines humanity adrift forever, a huge vessel of the living dead, and "Litanies for the Holy Virgin" speak for the sacred side.

The irreconcilable split between those equal and opposite passions—on the one hand for ether and orgy; on the other, for a closer relationship with God—made him feel a hypocrite and drove him, in his helplessness, to retreat to the Abbey of St-Benoît-sur-Loire. A photo taken in his tiny cell shows him slouched in a chair, hands folded, gazing reverently upward, showing the hint of a smile—in a rumpled swallow-tail tux with baggy striped pants, a vest and a collarless shirt, an outfit he might have had on at 5 o'-clock mass at Sacré-Coeur de Montmartre, drunk, chanting prayers, sobbing with guilty anguish after one of his nights in the dens of Montparnasse. Even then, after begging His mercy and forgiveness, he could say with a wink: "So once again God is fooled!" Though the remark might've been Max at his self-mocking best, it's no wonder some thought he was a Tartuffe, and even a close friend like Kahnweiler said he liked him but did not admire him.

At St-Benoît he tried to be more admirable. Leading a simple, ordered life, with no object for predatory urges and, thus, no arousal of ambivalence, he could concentrate on his relationship to God. "I am an evil seducer/ When I should be an apostle," he cries out in a poem that ends with the plea "Convert me! Convert me! Convert me!" He claimed he was haunted by devils, literally. *Infernal Visions* (1925) records those experiences in a series of prose poems, some of which, like "Achilles' Wheel" and "Hell Has Gradations," create a novel, macabre view of the dynamics of guilt.

Despite his self-tormenting obsessions, he was able to write moving lyrics ("Seascape at Roscoff," for example), semi-serious travel pieces ("Sunday in Marseilles" and "Antibes...") as well as flat-out comedy ("Jean Jacques," "The Best Girl"). The dialogue with God begins here, too, in the symposium series—comic only in that God speaks with a human voice, wryly. And there is no better example of the oscillation between "the burlesque and the mystical" (Michel Leiris' phrase) than the poem "On Death" that contains the line "you only go to Him trembling/ for your underwear's unbelievably foul."

Still, after seven years' stay, he decided to give city life one more try, settling in at the Hotel Nollet. Here, surrounded by a close group of writers and composers that included dear old friends Cocteau and Henri Sauguet, he indulged his thirst for pleasure one last time, always, as he said jokingly, "too sensual" for Cubism. He abandoned the Breton peasant outfit of butcher's coat and clogs for a return to his former luxuries: English tweeds, Hermès scarf, Sulka hat. And ether, the consumption of which, as Sauguet pointed out, attendance at mass did not affect.

Memoirs of this period mention his compelling eyes, seductive mouth and, as ever, the sinuous, non-stop brilliance of his conversation, Max shifting from comic to mystic, laughter to tears. Friends say he had a way of fixing his attention on someone, even a total stranger, making him feel important. He had time for everyone, high or low.

But only now, in his mid-50s, did he get a taste of the recognition he'd always said was denied him by "a conspiracy of silence" led by the Surrealists, jealous that his experiments had preceded theirs. He had some satisfaction in being made a member of the Legion d'Honneur and in seeing his earlier books republished, but every memoir that appeared diminished his part in the founding of Modernism, treating him as if he were a minor poet. The habit of regarding him as a distant second to Apollinaire—which originated with Apollinaire—became established. "I am in the Larousse," he grumbled, "and no one knows who I am."

At this time, too, he was writing "Ballad of the Night Visitor," his favorite among his own poems because of "the refined sincerity of the emotion . . . dressed up by a bit of adroit lying"—a clear reference to the fact that it was written about a man. It was a work whose shape he'd "foreseen and meditated on a long time." The repetitions of ballad form convey the narrator's frenzy, his "wild reasoning of madness" matched with the perfect backdrop, the beautiful moonlit severity of the frozen winter night that augments the intensity of his desire.

By 1938, when that poem appeared in *Ballades*, a collection that included five different books— the last that was published in his lifetime—Max was back at St-Benoît for good. He supported himself on book royalties and the sale of his paintings, entertaining visitors: Paul Eluard, the popular music-hall entertainer Charles Trenet, and Picasso, though their relationship was a dim shadow of what it had been, to Max's sorrow and Pablo's indifference. Max had finally given in completely to a life where it was enough to make art, write his memoirs, hear Mass said (twice a day), write letters, chop wood.

The poems of these years are increasingly devotional—meditative and penitent—focused on the sinner's relation to his God ("Ballad of the Perpetual Miracle," "The Restless Soul Remakes Heaven"); some chastise the unwary ("Infernal Visions" and "The Pilgrims at Emmaeus"); still others ("Death" and "Prophetic Dreams") concern his approaching end. But there are still plenty that have the old zany comic spirit of *The Dice Cup*, poems with abrupt, surprising changes of subject and mood that alter the reader's course, one sentence to the next ("Our Earthly Virtues Are But Castles in the Air," "Novel 1943" and—especially—"Magic Confession").

There are also the "yellow star" poems of this apostate Jew forced to wear the notorious armband. When the Nazis came for him, he received them with a martyr's calm and "a smile, as if it were no more than meaningless small talk." Even then, all lost, death staring him right in the eye, he could pun on the word "gestapo" ("*J'ai ta peau*": in the slang of this moment "Your ass is mine"). And his last gouache, left unfinished, is titled "Gestapo stuffing a parrot."

By this time, all his brothers and sisters, all his in-laws had been killed or were in the camps. "Burial at Quimper," written for his sister Delphine who died ("practically without an illness") after her husband had been executed, brings the poet full circle, back to the little boy reading Maupassant in summertime on the sagging balcony of the family home.

Which is still there, the way it's pictured in "The Novel," with two little windows above it that the Jacob children would look for on their way home from school. The family home, too, is just as he described it in "1914": chestnut trees on the quai in front of it, the prefecture across the Odet River, right up against Mt. Frugy, where he played tag and hide-and-seek and where, "in the midst of friends, instructed by angels/ I was unaware of myself and I wrote."

A century after Max Jacob left Quimper, a street, a bridge, a high school, even the courtyard of his house at 8, rue du Parc, all bear his name, a tribute to the hometown boy who made it big in the city. A few short blocks away is the Musée des Beaux-Arts where a room honoring him features drawings, manuscripts, paintings and a videotape that plays the story of his life on an endless loop.

Here, in the summer of 1994—and in Paris that fall at the Picasso Museum—to celebrate the 50th anniversary of his death, a state-sponsored exhibit was held detailing his long, complex relationship with Picasso, their conflicts and collaborations. In it, two things are for the first time completely clear: one is the enormous role Jacob played in fostering—better yet, in *embodying*—the Modernist spirit; the other is the breadth and brilliance of his achievement in the arts— as the premier avant-garde poet of his generation, as novelist, painter, critic, dramatist, literary theorist and aesthetician.

Why, then, the monumental neglect , the dismissiveness, the outright scorn? In death, as in life, he's seen as a distant second to Apollinaire, with whom he is usually billed "and Max Jacob" with barely a word about his work. Sancho Panza, "poor Max," "crazy Max." Has there been a conspiracy against him, as he always claimed? Recent evidence makes it clear that André Breton and his cohort *did* keep his work from being published in *Littérature*, the "official" Surrealist organ where the slogan "Read Reverdy, Don't Read Jacob," appeared. It's also possible that the conspiracy continued long after he was dead. When Louis Aragon was asked, late in his life, whether Max wasn't "writing Surrealist" long before others, he answered with striking disingenuousness that the term was not in use when *The Dice Cup* was published so he couldn't have!

Max was a chronic complainer, and he did needle, he did gossip, he was unsavory, maybe even hypocritical, too—though he once said he wasn't either as holy or as vicious as he was made to appear. But he *was* openly gay, at a time when almost no one came out, and an orgiast, especially fond of hairy cops and soldiers. And he *was* a Jew. Worse yet, a Jew who became a Christian, a Christian who then did the equivalent of committing himself—twice.

What really seems to bother critics and scholars most is the fact that he can't really be pinned down: is he serious or is he funny? And, if he's funny a lot, isn't this a dodge, a masquerade, a fear of exposure: hypersensitive Max playing peek-a-boo? And, if he shifts—as he does, characteristically—from serious to playful, isn't he just afraid of coming to grips with himself?

Readers should read Max and judge for themselves. What they will find is an enormously ambivalent human being who—we should be grateful for this—was willing to expose that ambivalence so we might identify with it, then acknowledge and accept our own. Jacob's recognition of our split nature accounts for the oscillation between the burlesque and the mystical, between his view of existence as absurd and his feeling that we live in "a universe whose nether sides are enchanted." It is time to recognize this fraught genius who knew, out of his own great suffering, that once we acknowledge our condition, we have no choice but to laugh.

Philadelphia, January 1999

Foreword to *The Dice Cup /*
Le cornet à dés

The poems that allude to war were written about 1909 and may be considered prophetic. They lack the tone our grief and sense of decency demand in poems about war: they date from an era that didn't know mass suffering. I foresaw the facts; I had no premonition of the horror.

1914

Doesn't lightning look the same to a foreigner? Someone who was at my parents' home was commenting on the color of the sky. Was that lightning? It was a pink cloud moving toward us. How everything changed! My God! Can it be your reality is so vibrant? The family home is there: the chestnut trees at the window, the prefecture right up against the chestnut trees, and Mt. Frugy right up against the prefecture, only its summit visible. A voice called out "God!" And there was light in the darkness. A huge body hid most of the landscape. Was it Him? Or Job? He was poor; his pierced flesh was showing, thighs covered by a scrap of cloth: what tears O Lord! he descended. . . How? Then couples larger than life descended too. They came from the air encased, in Easter eggs: they laughed and the balcony of our family home was littered with black threads like gunpowder. We were frightened. The couples set themselves up in our house while we watched through a window. For they were evil. There were even black threads on the dining room table where my brothers were taking apart Lebel cartridges. Since then, I've been watched by the police.

Le cornet à dés (1923)

1914

His swollen body is corseted in death. His plumed hat is flattened; his face a terrifying death mask, but so dark and savage you'd expect to see a rhino horn or an additional tooth in his fearsome jaw. Sinister vision of the German dead.

Le cornet à dés

War

Night: the outlying boulevards are full of snow. The muggers are soldiers; attacking with laughter and swords, they strip me of everything. I escape, only to end up in another square—is it a barracks square or an inn yard? All those sabres and lances. It's snowing. Someone sticks me with a needle: a poison to kill me! A death's head veiled in crêpe gnaws my finger. Dim streetlights cast my corpse's shadow on the snow.

Le cornet à dés

Memoirs of a Spy

The dog! To write to *Le Figaro* that I stole a gun! Him, the manager of the hotel. My brother forgot his gun at a hotel in Paris; the manager took it and told *Le Figaro* I did it. That shouldn't be hard to straighten out: send a letter care of "Dear orchestra critic, theatre page." But will that really help? I'm leaving that hotel. The bed's never made; the old maids come in and laugh at my misery; all the young ones know how to do is give you a peek at their shoulders. Did I ever steal a gun?

Le cornet à dés

Searching for the Traitor

Another hotel! My friend Paul is a prisoner of the Germans. O God, where is he? At the Lautenberg, on rue Saint-Sulpice, a hotel with furnished rooms, but I don't know his number. The hotel desk is a pulpit too high for my eyes. I'd like to, do you have a Miss Cypriani . . . it should be 21 or 26 or 28 and me wondering about the cabalistic significance of those numbers. With Paul a prisoner of the Germans because he betrayed his colonel. What era are we living in? 21 26 or 28 are in white on a black background with three keys. Who is Miss Cypriani? Another spy.

Le cornet à dés

The Key

When Milord Framboisy got back from the war, his wife scolded him royally in church, so he said: "Madame, here's the key to my entire fortune. I'm leaving forever." Out of a sense of delicacy, the lady let the key fall to the stone floor of the church. Over in a corner, a nun was praying because she'd lost her key, the one to the convent, and nobody could get in. "See if this will fit your lock." But the key was no longer there. It was already in the Cluny Museum: a huge key shaped like a tree trunk.

Le cornet à dés

1889–1916

In 1889, the trenches were sealed in wax and put under glass. Two thousand meters underground, two thousand Poles in chains didn't know what they were doing there. The French nearby discovered an Egyptian shield; they showed it to the world's greatest doctor, inventor of the ovariotomy. The world's greatest tenor sang two thousand notes in an auditorium two thousand meters around: he got paid two million and gave it to the Pasteur Institute. The French were under glass.

Le cornet à dés

Capital. Place-Setting

The young girl's breasts are too far apart; that should be taken care of in Paris; later on, it would look unrefined. But in Paris, all the shops are the same: gold and crystal! hat doctors! watch doctors! where are the breast doctors?

Le cornet à dés

The Feminist Question

Without admitting it, he was afraid she might some-
day get her animals wrong. When she arrived at the
foot of his tower, the frail romantic horsewoman
reined in her galloping steed, went inside, gave her fi-
ancé a massage, then whistled for her mount which
had wandered off but came back to her. That Made-
moiselle de Valombreuse was a masseuse, her fiancé
easily forgave, but that she could subdue a beast, that
was just too much.

Le cornet à dés

La Rue Ravignan

"You can't bathe in the same river twice," said the philosopher Heraclitus. But here it's always the same ones climbing the street! Happy or sad, they go by at the same times. I've named all of you who walk the rue Ravignan for famous dead people. Here's Agamemnon. There's Mme. Hanska! Ulysses is the milkman! Patroclus lives down the street and a Pharoah is next door. Castor and Pollux are the ladies on the fifth floor. But you, old ragman, who come to take the still-unspoiled scraps in the magic morning when I'm turning off my good big lamp, you that I don't know, mysterious, poor ragpicker, I've given you a celebrated name: I call you Dostoevsky!

Le cornet à dés

Moon Poem

At night three mushrooms are the moon. Abruptly as a cuckoo clock striking, they rearrange themselves each month at midnight. In the garden are rare flowers, little men lying down, a hundred of them, reflections in a mirror. In my dark room a luminescent censer is prowling, then two . . . phosphorescent airships, reflections in a mirror. In my head a bee is talking.

Le cornet à dés

Frontispiece

Yes, it fell from my nipple and I wasn't aware of it. The way a boat and its crew glide out of their anchorage in the rocks without even a ripple, without the earth sensing that new adventure, a new poem fell from my Cybele-breast and I wasn't aware of it.

Le cornet à dés

Poem

To erase the heads of the generals of the empire! But they're still alive. All I can do is change their hats: which are full of gun-cotton, and these gentlemen of the Empire are not amused—gun-cotton is flammable. I didn't realize it was so dove-white. To enter that Biblical landscape! But it's a woodcut: a row of houses of different heights, a shoreline behind a trickle of water, a trickle of water behind a palm tree. Which is an illustration for *Saint Matorel*, the Max Jacob novel. Miss Leonie and I took a walk there; I didn't know people in that book carried suitcases! The generals seated at the table with their hats on were alive, but doesn't that mean Miss Leonie and I are, too? I can't enter that Biblical landscape, it's a woodcut—I even know the engraver. When their hats were back on the heads of the generals of the Empire, everything was where it should be. I re-entered the woodcut and peace reigned in the desert of art.

Le cornet à dés

In the Background

It's an outing in the country, a little group around a well. The poor child is alone on the shore, on rocks jutting out from the dune and she seems to have a halo around her head. Oh, I'll be able to save her, all right! Me, the big fat guy, here I come running. Over by the well they're playing the Marseillaise and I'm rushing off to save her. I still haven't mentioned the color of the sky because I couldn't be sure it didn't make with the sea a continuous color like a slate blackboard smeared with chalk; yes, a diagonal streak of chalk like the blade of a guillotine.

Le cornet à dés

In Hill Country

I came to a hill that was meadowland all the way to a tree-lined summit from which other hills could be seen. At the hotel I saw my father who told me: "I had you come here so I could marry you off." "But I don't have a black suit." "Meaningless. The main thing is you're going to get married." On the way to the church, I saw my intended, a pale young woman. That afternoon I was struck by the charm of the festivities. The meadow was ringed with tables and chairs. Couples came, noblemen, scholars, school friends, sitting in the hollows, under the trees. I had a sudden urge to paint it. But what about my wife? That was just a joke, right? Nobody marries a man who's not wearing a black suit, the way the English do. At the meadow the mayor, also principal of the elementary school, made a speech saying the marriage had been called off because they'd learned the state of my finances. Then, choking back sobs of humiliation, I wrote this piece, but with lots of absurd literary flourishes.

Le cornet à dés

The Novel

There's only been one cozy little place in my life: the one in Quimper with two little windows opening onto a balcony. On our way home from school we'd watch for them. One day, as revenge for a practical joke, someone threw ink out the window onto my raincoat. Violet stains! What a dirty trick! I grabbed the wrist of the perpetrator and dragged outside by her hips a woman in a dressing gown. Someday that woman would be mine.

Le cornet à dés

Literature and Poetry

We strolled in the brilliant sunshine near Lorient, watching all through those September days as the ocean rose higher and higher, covering the woods, the land, the cliffs. Soon there was nothing in the way of the blue sea but the winding paths and the families huddled close together. A sad-looking child in a sailor suit was with us. He held my hand: "Monsieur," he said, "I've been to Naples; did you know there are many little streets where you can be alone and no one sees you; it's not that there are so many people in Naples but there are so many little streets everyone has his own." "What lies is this little one telling now?" said the father. "He's never been to Naples." "Monsieur, your son is a poet." "That's fine with me, but if he winds up being a literary man I'll wring his neck!" The twists and turns of the path left drying by the sea had made him think of Naples.

Le cornet à dés

Literary Standards

A dealer in Havana sent me a cigar wrapped in gold which had been smoked a little. The poets sitting with me said he'd done it to mock me, but the old Chinese who was our host said it was the custom in Havana when one wished to show great honor. I brought out two magnificent poems a scholar friend had written down translations of for me because I admired them when I heard them read. The poets said they were well-known and worthless. The old Chinese said they couldn't have known the poems because they only existed in a single manuscript copy in Pehlvi, a language they didn't know. Then the poets started laughing loudly like children while the old Chinese gazed at us sadly.

Le cornet à dés

A Bit of Art Criticism

Jacques Claess is indeed a name for a Dutch painter. Let us, if you will, cast a glance at his origins. Little Jacques' mother, as she herself confessed, bleached her face with vinegar, which explains why the paintings of the master have a varnished look. In Jacques' village, on St. Roofer's Day, it was the custom of the roofers to let themselves drop from the rooftops without crushing the pedestrians; and they also had to throw their ropes from the sidewalk to the chimney. The whole thing very picturesque, which must certainly have given our painter his taste for the picturesque.

Le cornet à dés

My Life

The town to be captured is in a room. The spoils aren't heavy and the enemy won't carry them off because it doesn't need money since this is a story and only a story. The town has painted wood ramparts: we cut them out and paste them in our book. There are two chapters or parts. Here's a red king with a gold crown climbing onto a saw. That's Chapter II; as for Chapter I, I can't remember it.

Le cornet à dés

Biographical

Already, at the age of three, the author of these lines was remarkable: he had done a terra-cotta passe-boule* of his concierge at the moment that she, with tears in her eyes, was plucking a bird. The bird stuck out its futile neck. But it was not that passe-boule, just a pastime. All in all, it's remarkable that he hadn't been remarked upon: remarkable, though not regrettable, because if he had been remarked upon, he wouldn't have become remarkable; his career would've ended, which would have been regrettable. It's remarkable that it might have been regretted and regrettable that it might have been remarked. The bird in the passe-boule was a goose.

Le cornet à dés

type of cartoon in which a huge, distorted mouth is pictured wide-open, catching a ball.

Father Unknown

There's the bull of Europa and Io's cow; I'm the son of an ox. My mother was a shepherdess so you can guess the rest.

At a gala event in London I thought I'd make a splash by coming with my father and mother. What a triumph! Suddenly I decided to try the stage: so I left the hat trade and my wife. Result: I'm sitting on a bench on Rochechouard Boulevard, my collar up. When the police ask me my father's name and I answer "There's the bull of Europa, Io's cow, I'm the son of an ox" they take me down to the station. It's not a crime to find out who one's father is but it is to lie to the police.

in "Les soirées de Paris" (1913)

Life of the Party

That's me, the jolly one, life of the party. Tiny glasses and a moustache stop me dead every time, and not seeing my name on a letter not addressed to me shocks and hurts. But if you get a circle dance going, I'll be singing and dancing at the same time. Recently, I was singing "The Little Hunchback" in a farandole when I noticed one was there. I wondered if I should stop or go on. I had the good sense not to sing every verse. Yes, that's me, the jolly one, life of the party.

in "Les soirées de Paris"

The Concarneau Regatta

The drowning don't always go straight to the bottom. And all someone struggling in the water has to remember is he can swim and he's watching his pants leg flop like a jumping jack. That's what happened to me at the Concarneau Regatta. I was perfectly relaxed before I sank, at least that's how the swells going by in their skiffs will note my efforts . . . in short, a certain optimism. The shore so near! With people of the Jewish persuasion life-size and so very gracious. What surprised me as I came out of the water is that I wasn't all that wet and was seen not as a poodle but as a man.

Le cornet à dés

Let's Bring Back the Old Themes

In the village where public sales of paintings are held in a courtyard, with frames right on the ground, the three-hundred-plus windows their owners had rented were crowded with butchers. It was like a public execution! Everyone there to witness the slaughter of art and happiness. Some of the butchers had binoculars.

Le cornet à dés

Sir Elizabeth (Pronounced *Soeur*)

The town of Happney was destroyed, alas! Nothing left but a wall between a pair of square towers that look like farm buildings or cisterns. Once they were schools: now they're empty. Nothing left . . . nothing but a stable door full of cracks. And the pavement covered with brambles. But the station master's still there, he's the one who told me the story of Sir Elizabeth a female but she had to dress like a male. Sir Elizabeth was entered in a poetry contest. At that time, in America, females didn't think of becoming poets. Sir Elizabeth was crowned and had the right to a double profile, one on either side of a stable door. The door is still standing; the two busts have been, alas, damaged by time. Sir Elizabeth was aroused by the sculptor who was doing her bust and she revealed her sex to him, but the sculptor rejected her because she'd tricked the town. At that point, Sir Elizabeth joined the military and was killed.

Le cornet à dés

Errors of Mercy

I'll go to prison with him rather than see him get away. And it was done! We're in a massive tower. One night in my sleep I reached out to restrain him and touched nothing but a white foot on its way to the ceiling. Now I'm alone here by a window in the tower. From the top of their massive haywagons the peasants gaze at me with merciful eyes.

Le cornet à dés

The Two Elite Audiences

The day of the great steeplechase, the queen-mother wore blue velvet stockings. One of the king's mistresses came up to him at the grandstand: "Prince, that woman is not your mother; she has no right to the throne whose prerogatives she usurps!" In a long speech, the king praised prostitution then married the mistress, a prostitute. A servant wearing glasses who slept in the kitchen on the top of an ornamented porcelain stove was pleased with the marriage. What do the elites think? The audience of first-nighters thought the speech on prostitution was too long, while the other elite audience applauded it warmly.

Le cornet à dés

Poem

"Madame, I'll be on your doorstep every morning till your son the captain returns from the colonies."

"If you want to see him that badly, it'd be a lot easier to check the directories to find out what day he gets back."

We'd gone to the lady's house when she was out. My sister swore she had a beautiful piece of furniture: a bed with ivory inlays whose inlays were falling out.

"You see beds like this everywhere. Besides, it's not beautiful if it's not old, and it's not old seeing as there's an inlay of a picture of the lady's son. And don't use the lady's nail file. First, because you don't know how to use nail files when they're made of ivory, and also because you don't use ladies' nail files when they aren't here."

"I'll tell her I'm waiting for her son the captain in the colonies."

"She'll think you're abusing her hospitality, send you packing, and you'll be back drinking out on the sidewalk by yourself."

Le cornet à dés

from The Cock and the Pearl

I thought he was bankrupt, but he still had slaves and several rooms in his house. On the rocks, opera singers were half-naked in their bathing suits. In the evening, we got into coaches and the little trains slipped beneath the pines. And I thought he was bankrupt! . . . he even found me an editor who gave me a turtle with a glossy pink shell. I'd have been better off with even a dime.

*

I declare myself world-famous, oviparous, a giraffe, altered, a sinophobe and hemispheric. I quench my thirst at springs in the atmosphere that laugh concentrically and fart at my uncertainty.

*

White arms become my entire horizon.

*

A picture of grandpa by a five-year-old: an ox's head smoking a pipe. The family's delighted; grandpa's riled.

*

When you paint a picture, it completely changes with each brushstroke, turning like a cylinder, almost interminably. When it stops turning, it's finished. My latest was a Tower of Babel made of lighted candles.

*

Monsieur de Max showed each of the two sides of his profile to each of the two parties in turn as if they were so many giant prisms.

*

Augustine was a farm girl when the President noticed her. To avoid scandal, he gave her titles and teaching certificates making her a governess, then a "de" in front of her name, some money, and the more he gave her, the more worthy of him she became. I, a poor Breton peasant, have given myself everything: the title of duke, the right to wear a monocle, I was even able to increase my height and expand my thought, but I still can't be worthy of myself.

*

Huge fruit on a dwarf tree, much too big for it. A palace on the rock of an island too-small. An art in a nation too pure for it.

*

A dancing bear left the town square and went to piss against a wall.

*

It happens when you exhale that the material world wakes up the other one.

*

Coming down the rue de Rennes I bit into my *pain rustique* with such feeling it felt like I was tearing up my heart.

*

The infant, the effluent, the elephant, the frog and the fried potato.

*

If you give a magician a piece of clothing, he can tell you who wore it; when I put on my shirt, I can tell you what I was thinking the day before.

*

Its flowers are like a forget-me-not's, arranged so you'd think the green part is a clown making a candelabra with his arms, one foot backward.

*

A dog barks before dawn; the angels begin whispering to shush him.

*

Stained ceilings are symbolic of the life of their houses' inhabitants. See the two bears reading the paper by a fire.

*

I rented a Pierrot costume made of percale, with pants that didn't even reach the knee, fighting over it with a certain sergeant. I found letters in it. Yes! letters I'm going to publish when the shop's demolished or the sergeant's dead.

*

Struck by lightning, the archangel only had time to untie his tie; it looked like he was still praying.

*

Fog, spiderweb.

*

The jet from an inkbottle makes a big splash! It's no frog, just a little conductor pointing to the footlights and the hem of a white dress.

*

The ballet brought back to reality: victorias with scarlet wheels, howitzers, the crowd, but especially the sky! the sky! a real sky! reality brought back to the ballet.

*

At the foot of the bed, the mirrored armoire, a guillotine. Our two guilty heads visible.

*

To get revenge on the writer who gave them life, the heroes he created hide his penholder.

*

You mountains like the foam on a pot of boiling milk under that airship from where, as from a huge dice cup, the Good Natured old globe appears, the forehead of Father Doublesphere.

Le cornet à dés

Allusion to a Circus Act

"**K**eep your back straight!" The marquess is a cowboy; the columns of pines resemble old ruins. All the birds in the sky (there is no sky) fly towards her musketeer hat as if to the sea. And this took place in New England! A young, blond-haired man, a little too-well got up in hunting costume, complains he hasn't eaten for sixteen hours. The marquess won't feed him those little island birds: she'll lead him to a grotto where he can take his boots off.

Le cornet à dés

Sad Last Appeal to the Phantoms Inspirations from the Past

I was born near a racetrack where I saw horses run beneath the trees. My trees! My horses! because all that was for me. I was born near a racetrack. My childhood traced my name in the bark of the chestnuts and beeches. My trees are now nothing more than the white feathers of a bird crying "Leon! Leon!" Vague memories of sumptuous chestnuts where as a child I inscribed my grandfather's name. Vague memories of races! jockeys! now seen from this distance nothing more than pathetic toys. The horses no longer noble my jockeys' helmets black. Go, turn, turn away, imprisoned thoughts that will never fly. The symbol that suits you isn't the lithe gallop of jockeys on the green, but some dusty bas-relief hiding from my grief those chestnuts of autumn where my grandfather's name is written.

Le cornet à dés

The Tough Guy's Lament

It's summer again the blinds closed tight
Blinds the roses miss
Those big white fish on the sheet of glass
Sweet Catherine and my buddy Nicholas!
The sun on the pond at the gas works
It's the sickness of love
And all my desires that keep me here
With demons and daughters of the street

So let's pour one down our throats
While another drunk floats up into the van

Le laboratoire central (1921)

Leon! Leon!

Straw in the forests the sound of footsteps
My fat cousin in a room
Tell me what it's all about!
I don't have the courage to put my other shoe on.
The only real good-byes are in prison.
I see crowns in the stars
And apocalyptic halos for the hares of Uranus
The fire in the woodstove roars at death
Leon! Leon! it's like that every night
Clock feet fly-torturing
Troops in the houses, the poor, alone, in the streets
I'll drive a nail into your hand armchair arm
And a nail into your other hand
Nails into your board feet
And I'll whack you empress Eudoxia
I can't stop you
Is he crying?
Messenger angels wear pale blue caps
Averroes! is he a hero? A hero is he, Averroes?
How to gloss over my weakness
I who am always *au courant*
If not with that charming word
Refinement!

Le laboratoire central

Poem

To hurl a wing at that pearl: a helmet,
To reach the sky on its fiery decline
And the serpent flew to South Africa
Two dragons struggled for the conquest of Max
Above a convent full of troubled monks
Twenty wild mushrooms resembling marquises
Having shown their big white-pantalooned feet
Sure, heaven knows me! You have to realize that
But what difference does it make while we're alive
I was, as a student, intimate with my professors
They brought me exotic bonbon-colored drawings
I kept them the way you keep violets
Quadrilles! I danced with my sister's child
All dressed up on my shoulder or my head
At my aunt's they put my bed in the parlor
And I didn't get up till noon or later
Her son complained my cigars were a luxury
Here's the cliff edge where my tree grew
There's an amphitheatre full of young girls pink and
    white
I lay down at the edge and read books
My youthful thoughts were dressed in their Sunday
    best
Wearing flowers in their soft hair
I'm one of the escapees from the prison at Nantes
A child recognized our tonsured foreheads
When we asked him the way to Clisson

When the serving nuns made their deposition before
   God
The trees, the sun, the mill, the torrent
Were a stairway from my convent at Nantes
Hiding the shame of my prison life

Le laboratoire central

Absurd Metamorphosis

The wicker flask like a thousand yellow flowers the
   goblet
Where the wine, the blood of Christ, is.
The wicker basket becomes a suitcase
A flying bag
With points at either end
It won't sit still it flies away.
Now there's this terrace, a balcony on rue St-Denis
A dealer's: with junk, butterfly nets
Gas cans, all outside.
The pilot in the suitcase lands
All bottled up in the big flask
"Open up! Let me out!"—"Where'd you come from?"
"I went off to war a corporal. Now I'm a general."
"You put holes in these nets
And upset my pots and pans
I want three hundred bucks for damages!"

Le laboratoire central

A View in Perspective

Mountain view of the turreted white house
It's dark, with one lighted window
And two turrets, two turtledove turrets.
Behind the window in the house
Is the fiery light of love!
Plenty of it, winged, eloquent.
On the third story
In another room
Unlit, lies a dead man
And all the sorrow of death,
Sorrow's plenty,
Sorrow's wings,
Sorrow's eloquence
View in perspective of a turreted white house.

Le laboratoire central

Playing the Horn

The three ladies playing the horn
In their bathroom late at night
Have a serious jerk for a teacher
Who's only there in the daylight

The fair-haired fellow
Catching crabs with his hands
Doesn't say a word
He's illegitimate

Three mothers for that bald child
When one would be plenty
His father's a big-shot but he's poor
And treats him like a bad penny

(Signature)

Heart of the muses, you're blinding me
It's me you see winding his horn
On the Iena bridge on Sunday
With a sign on my sleeve.

Le laboratoire central

To Mr. Modigliani to Prove I'm a Poet

A cloud is a postman between continents
A primer on exile that the seas,
Doomed by hell to tearful combat,
Will not spell out on the sheen of space.
Dark mountain tops sleep on terraces
Furrows plowed by God to hide humans in
Without reading the secret in the passing cloud
Who no longer knows what he's carrying
Though sometimes when his enemy the wind chases
    him
He turns and roars hurling a bronze foot.
As a child, I was gifted. A thousand lights from the sky
Moved the wakened spell of my dreams
Eclipsing the banner of the real.
In the midst of friends, instructed by angels,
I was unaware of myself and I wrote.
Instead of a woman, one day I met God
Companion who graces me
Though I cannot know Him.
He is my peace and my happiness
He makes me feel secure
And to celebrate his mysteries
He made me his secretary.
Every night I decipher
Sheets of paper filled with numbers

He writes with his own hand
And places in my mind.
In the aquarium of the air live inquisitive demons
Who collapse the cloud to steal our secret from it.

Le laboratoire central

Watered Earth

So much is hidden
In the green mist of dawn! So much joy
And misery. In the evening mist
The rose not even gone
And the dog's already bored and yawning.
In the woods as many birds as leaves.

At night thinking of poetry
I just can't sleep
Morning dew
Don't scatter my words
"You'll find them in the street
On the way to see your friends:
Between the great sad sky and everything full of yearn-
    ing
The miracle will arise from the watered earth."

Le laboratoire central

Festival

The Order of the Rainbow to decorate the night.
A palace of diamonds like lumbar vertebrae.
I sat at the edge of a merry crowd
With five bored women hothouse flowers
Whose eyes flashed furious at missing dessert
Heads twisting as a new guest arrived.
The terrace bright as fireworks
Full of dancing and fiery duels.
Inside on gorgeous divans people in costume
And Hindus with jewels embedded in their flesh
—None readier than they for the great adventure—
Awaited the impossible.
"Let's see your nails"—"Too bad they aren't pretty"
"And this line means your future's sad."
While elsewhere others did the dance of the nails
    motionless
Their hands flickering like stars.
I said to the fortune-teller: "What a marvel you are!
You've listed my woes so marvelously!"
Two of Balzac's heroes with amphibians' backs
Who entered my spine while my palm was being read
Said: "You shouldn't play with yourself in bed!"

Le laboratoire central

Malachites

Friends came visiting merry and gay
Down the wood-road from the mountain
A little noble from the Gotha Almanac
      Who was black
A writer and a bureaucrat, a dancer from the Opera.
Reflected in the mirrors
They discussed the dancer's pain
Recommending camphor and phosphorus
All six of us except the black
Dined on cadavers
With salt and pepper
Oil and vinegar
While he ate cooked flowers
With a dash of holy water
From a bowl.
Under the veranda made of sand
Yellow sand and myrtle
The writer played upon his flute
And conjured up the devil.

Le laboratoire central

74

Other Characters at the Masked Ball

Tumult of horses, the mikado's war
Wild rose on gold background
Maybe a gift
From my last lover
Hanging from my arm
He loves me strikingly
Violation, viola, violin, I'm the ultra-violet
Leaving for Chicago
I'll be black and blue in coach

Le laboratoire central

Other Characters at the Masked Ball

THE BLIND WOMAN

The blind woman with the bloody eyes chooses her
    words
Speaking to no one of her ills

She has hair like moss
She wears jewels and reddish stones

The fat blind woman with the bloody eyes
Writes polite letters with margins and space between
    the lines

She's careful how her velvet dress is folded
Strives to make it something more

And if I haven't mentioned her brother-in-law
It's because now that young man is out of favor

Because he gets drunk and gets the blind woman
    drunk
Who laughs, who laughs then moos

Le laboratoire central

Menage of Godless Artists

Magician who moves men in photographs around
Makes horseless carriages depart
Could you also run a file across
The evil nature of my bastard child?
The church could, but the Devil says no.
Paris, you magnificent city
With your trees untrimmed
The Republic has failed
To combat him
Whose empire depends on the hindmost

Twined snakes formed my initials
On linens hung behind the hospital
They were also read in music scales
And girls braided them in their pigtails
Their downstrokes give you shade, my Trocadero
And support your empty mezzanine, o Metro
But every evening draws me to the hearth
I have my wife and her dog: I hear him bark.

Le laboratoire central

Glass of Blood

for Juan Gris

Our ideas at Brocken* our hearts at Calvary
The ones the color of time
The others of blood
I drank half a glass of your blood
Threw the rest into the sea
Where it gave birth to a big ship
With an acrobat in green
At the top of the stern mast
All the dead were moaning in the shape of waves
While the damned braced themselves against the black
 rocks
The cries of the living intertwined with seaweed
The horrible joyous the still more horrible sad
In the hold as in the prisons in '93
The weary, performing dogs and officers
The women crafty and sad
The fatal sound of the waves at the fringe
While humanity played cards on the ship
A minister of state read his destiny in them
On the stern.
What good all the blood shed on Calvary
For this ship rising on the waves of the dead?
We must suffer since we must to live we must to see
The bloodstain reaches the rocks shuddering
Like my lyre
While the ship bears all humanity
I know a shop colored by the Savior's blood

But the frantic "successor"
Has planted a flag of the same color there
Today the sky is red with the blood of Christ
But in flower-filled Luxembourg**
A wild boar flushed from the trees
Has flung his gold horns and his fury
At me, terrified against a marble vase.
Tomorrow winter will come nasturtiums fade
And I will dream, Lord, that you've been murdered.
The northern air has healed the wounds.

Le laboratoire central

*the legendary home of Walpurgisnacht
**the famed gardens of Montparnasse

Litanies for the Holy Virgin

Virgin so wonderfully bright reflecting the light of the
Holy Spirit
Virgin so like Heaven Heaven married her
The Lord's only mother possible
Child of fifteen who spoke to an angel
Honored by marriage to God
Honored by mothering God
Mother and spouse of Heaven
Miracle one, miraculous
Guardian of the sole treasure
Guardian of earth's treasure
Guardian of the heavenly treasure
Mother of hope and anguish
Entrails deified
Providence of God
Providence of men
Shepherd of the Pascal Lamb
Mother who watched the Man grow
Mother who watched Him suffer
Mother who watched Him die
Mother confident, marveling
Eternal empress of Christians
Empress in the court of the perfect
Humble empress
Intangible, attentive, feeling, just, wise and pure
Stairway to perfection
Throne of perfection
Caretaker of souls

Lamp of our vigils
President of our assemblies
Nurse of our weaknesses
Needle-colored robe
All to each everything to each
Emerald of the heavens
Diamond of nights
Topaz of days
Mother of the Word, strength of Genius, muse of the
    arts,
Life of thought, thought of life
Evermore young girl
Evermore young mother
Purity forever
Beauty
Save the souls of my friends killed in the war

Le laboratoire central

Warning!

No light in the room! no door or window! He lies there suffering in every part of his poor body. No hope of any help, of the slightest relief. Not even that he'll die from his disease. No end to this pitch-black room, this unbearable illness, this howling like a woman in labor.

Visions infernales (1924)

Demons as I Rise

I know you, the one from yesterday, and all the others. Your eye's a little listless today. Yesterday it was colder, more malevolent. No, no! These aren't the great visions: Beethoven with a red blotch on his face, the convent gardener who gnaws his upper lip and bears the three spots of madness on his ears and forehead. It's not them! not him! it's the little man with a head no bigger than a fist. Stupid, crass and wicked, these little demons of morning.

Visions infernales

Hell Has Gradations

When I was working at the Fashion Cooperative I tried, despite the watchful eye of the dark, ugly old maid, to steal a pair of suspenders. I got chased down those splendid stairs not for the theft, but because I was a lazy worker who hated mindless finery. You descend, they follow. The stairs are less beautiful down by the offices than in the public area. They are less beautiful in shipping and handling than at the office level. They are even less beautiful down in the cellar! But what can I say about the swamp I came to? About the laughter? The animals I brushed against and the murmur of invisible things? The water turned into fire, my fear into a blackout. When I came to, I was in the hands of silent, unnamable surgeons.

Visions infernales

Achilles' Wheel

Neither the jaws of the rocks with their purple gums nor the snide laughter of the holly that gnaws them and would gladly gnaw anything else can faze the bicycle thief; these slabs of rock are great springboards. Everything warns the thief, but he has confidence in the two gleaming half-dollars carrying him. He doesn't listen to the voices from the past, the vale of the past, or those on the path or in his conscience. He is stopped only in the face of this: a chasm the moving wall of jaws with purple gums is pushing him towards. No way out! he must get off the machine. Get down somewhere else. But where? And what I hear is a huge laugh, big as nature itself. He has reached his destination: the abyss!

Visions infernales

First Symposium

The sweetness of loving God so sweet
who slips up beside us like velvet:

"You don't say you love me very often."

"Lord, your words are harsh."

"That's because I'm jealous. Give me your pen
and ink and stop writing."

"We're both here. There's only You and I on
earth."

"You've been waiting for me a long time!"

"You were behind the curtain: I knew it all
along, Lord."

"Your belief in me comes so easily you forget
to love me for it. Don't be fooled. Meditate on my at-
tributes. Let that be your only aim."

"Lord, I'm intoxicated by you and my youth."

"I hear you dying with love for me."

"Lord you are a treasure no one can take away
from me. When I give myself to you, I'm afraid I'll lose
my mind."

"It's time for mind to lose you."

Fond de l'eau (1927)

Second Symposium

"**W**hat work have you done?"

"What has been worthy of recognition, I fear, Lord."

"Since it's me you've put your hope in, show me some gratitude."

"I've never thought of money except to give it to you."

"And to entertain you?"

"To suffer in another way? should I imagine a Paradise that would not fill me with You? I know You, and You alone can move me: nearness to God! survival of the self, separate, united. This I believe."

"You're a prophet?"

"Who says that? . . . Lord make me die so I can stop sinning."

"The end is near. I'll give you ears of corn when you can hear me better."

Fond de l'eau

Third Symposium

"Look at me. Are you scared?"

"What are those little flames around Your Face? Lord, if you were only as proud of me as I am of You."

"You're too full of life. An amethyst is the color of night; be like one. You won't go wrong."

"I've warmed with my hands which are spirit the bird which is the Holy Spirit."

"Put the bird on the marble base of Truth."

"I love the me in You."

"You love the me in you."

Fond de l'eau

On Death

Earth is just a mezzanine
hardly thirty-six floors
between cellar and attic.
Under the courtyard garden
the flagstones of the kitchen floor
are your uncle and your late cousin
the flames are their water
black coal their tub
the attic all saints and angels.
You're simply dying for God
but you only go to Him trembling
for your underwear's unbelievably foul
and you lack the guile
to intrigue for His most holy grace.
Will you be here beside me when
I'm dying, Mercy?
Or will you leave me in the darkness
when the black ocean pays its call . . .
My days! what regrets! harp strings
tuned by God or candles
the last of which he snuffs.
(If only they'd been days instead of nights!)
Looking back,
I see the loose ends of the years.
Goodbye to the entire earthly cavalcade,
my secret angel's here
and the two doors to the end:
sweet dawn or everlasting stench.

Fond de l'eau

Shore

I complain like a flute
Always the same key
The frog in the watercress
Sounding his C
Would prefer a bassoon.

My little elves the multitudes outsmart
Will I have to all my life
Go back to bed
Dreaming of a greater art?

So many faces so many stations
But never some consideration
For the poor sap a snowstorm
Catches in its trap.

Rivage (1931)

Seascape at Roscoff

Sky and sea the color of a blackboard
after the chalk is erased!
There's a boatman on the opposite shore
near the little hotel on the point.
The sea is deep and dark,
rocks too steep and slick for landing
the light screened by clouds.
The ground rises and falls . . . What's going on
in the shimmering folds
who's roaming those deserted cones
"I can hear you even when you aren't speaking."
A dark cape! A green sentry box!
night soon: the sea will be harsh.

Les pénitents en maillots roses (1925)

Jean Jacques

Jean Jacques drags a hermit
from the woods deep and dark
he wants to find a home for him
near his own hearth

While they're botanizing
in the bush he catches sight of
one of the twenty-eight shirts of his
a thief has kept in hiding

A hare making a delivery
goes between two manzanillas
Rousseau's thinking of Italy
while the hermit says novenas

I love to sing romances
in the back of my canoe
and in the woods beneath the branches
watch the river flow.

Les pénitents en maillots roses

The Best Girl

Having made it all the way
To Paris from Bourget
From there to the Canaries
The plane relands at Nice
Pale and suffering from jaundice
Not raised eyebrows O Japan
Or kimonos can maroon us!
So let's let Old Maloney
Go and populate Dahomey,
Dona Maria Pilar
Majorca the Balearic,
While I to the steppes of Russia
Fly to meet Natasha.
Ethelka from Kamchatka
Made a gift of a *couronne*
She made in Bouches-du-Rhône
Ethelka, Jeanne and Paula
Are exciting to recall.
But the best of them is Suzy,
Sixty-five rue de Buci.

Rivage

Travels

The style of modern poetry being ideally suited to recording impressions of travel—no doubt because poets are travellers to begin with—we are borrowing it for ours.

ANTIBES AND THE ANTIBES ROAD

The factory on Jujube
old street in Antibes
with its four thousand inhabitants—a panoramic view
from the Italian stairs asthmatics climb with ease
The Vauban fort looks like a ship
The Gothic church spire lustrous as wax
Shadows of nets mended under sycamores
spreading like water on the children's faces
In spite of the fortress and the ancient implements of
    war
the gentlemen officers and enlisted men
who've grown soft in this mild climate
lack you might say that military bearing
—but what do I know!—
Yet tell me where the barracks are
Beyond the hills I see grape vines alfalfa
blue sea below the ramparts
a town proud its water comes from Roman fountains
I'd bet there's even a casino
but no barracks
none at all.
So tell me, Antibes, where you put your troops.
Will they be sleeping in the olive groves tonight?

in that theatre the size of a Louis Quinze attic?
or does each man have a lady friend
he shares a bed with at the mayor's the saddler's the
 blacksmith's
the haberdasher's the garageman's or some other citi-
 zen's
(that's what I call billeting troops)
I want them, lured by the sand,
fighting with the crowning sea for a glimpse of blue
 sky,
to be carried off by their dream mares
mistaking manes for their sweethearts' hair
galloping to the moon's citadel of love
holding their ladies' necks and their horses'
in the same ardent lovers' grip
etc. . . . .etc. . . .etc. . . . (that's enough of Antibes)

Les pénitents en maillots roses

Sunday in Marseilles:
Prose Impressions

The skeleton of a port asleep on Sunday
and this giant old transatlantic liner
pitted with memories and rusted by time
Distant cliffs suggest the Adriatic
with its pink houses and umbrella pines
like a pearly smile behind a fan
I'm the lost child of these magnificent cities
what do I care if they're dancing in the cabaret
it's Sunday and the sea hidden by ships
can't console my democratic heart
Past overhanging warehouses and low-down dives
I've followed the waterfront long as a country mile
and that rusty giant of an old liner
dead from a kick by progress
to its folded wings
is perfectly suited to my weary orphan sadness
"No trespassing. No smoking."
Iron mysteries! poles with magnetic hooks
stationed at intervals like guards of the dock
Once they danced inside you, old ship
today you shut your portholes in royal fashion
against the violin sounds the sea hurls from the
    cabaret
What pride! and the bowl shape high up on your side.
And the sky that's everyone's! no masts just sky
that helps me, the child of these scientific cities,
understand my universe: port taxes guys miserable

at having to be the Sunday guardians of tons of dirty
 oil
The major business of a port is to take in each one
of those cargo ships arrogant in their knowledge of
 ocean spray
discharge their contents into our countryside
and hide the man who slept in his steel shelter be-
 tween-decks
under a boxcar's roof.
A port at dawn with its hundreds of pipes is no longer
a majestic sailing ship that cuts the golden water
offering its crossed arms like a temple of light
it's that iron hulk and those stone domes
the whore in Singapore already diseased
dock strikes with their bloodshed
signs jumbling the levels of the sky!
Now the blue mountains were floating like airplanes
and men in pince-nez leaning on their canes
watched the workers eating raw fish
streetcar drivers romancing women
with onyx eyes and honey-colored skin
Proprietors pleasant but detached
"Payment required in advance"
The black and the Japanese eating from faience
out of the office an aria soaring loud
Flirting with the waitress is allowed

Les pénitents en maillots roses

Ballad of the Night Visitor

What a winter that one of 1929 was! Paris in white velvet, all the windows like moonstones.

That night, that December night, I woke up in my cozy room in the Hotel Nollet with the wild reasoning of madness. In my cozy room, I dressed warmly in thick wool clothing because of the cold (it was about 2 a.m.) in good thick gloves and the wild reasoning of madness.

"Where are you going at this time of night, in the cold, darkness and snow?" asked the night watchman. "You'll never find a taxi."
"I'm going to the Cirque du Temple, watchman." What a winter that one of 1929 was. Paris in white velvet, all the windows like moonstones, and every street: light and shadow.

"Let's go, my poor numb driver, 108 Boulevard du Temple, please."
It was the only taxi running in Paris at that time of night in the pristine snow, at that pristine time of night. And how it had snowed! Then my feverish eyes, full of mystical apparition, gazed at your window, where you slept, I on a snow-covered bench and your window, your window like a moonstone.

"Are you a sleepwalker?" asked the driver anxiously, "because you don't look like a thief." Her house was before me with its window like all the windows: pearl, mica or moonstone. Then, in a dream or a smile, like an angel descended from paradise just for her, I went to touch her house—your gloves! take off your gloves!—then her door.

The taxi brought, then took back a man almost unconscious with joy, with the cold, with love, crying tears of joy, of love, of cold, of love, a man in tears.

"Already?" said the night watchman of the Hotel Nollet almost asleep that night. Whether it was a mechanical doll, a hypnotized victim . . . he climbed the quaint narrow stairs, decorated with a light switch . . . Whether it was I . . . or she in me . . . I don't know who it was: me? she in me? She, I saw her day and night, but not every day and night, and she knew nothing of that night visit at the white wall, at the oak door, in that Paris of white velvet and moonstone, light and shadow in every street . . . knew nothing of that visit.

After my love had died, O for long months after, the sorrow and the joy of having loved (do I still love you?), after the dark charnel house of bloody severing and you dead and I dead and you in me and I in you, and you dead and I dead, I here and you there, I spoke to you, my angel, I told you of my visit in the snow to your doorstep in that Paris of white velvet and moonstone, light and shadow in every street.

"I knew you were crazy because as any doctor will tell you, the really craziest are the calmest."

And you dead and I dead, and you in me and I in you, and you dead and I dead, I here and you there.

Ballades (1938)

The Balcony of Romeo and Juliet

That's the balcony of the military bandstand! Oh, I know the band's flutist well. And I knew Eugenia, the doctor's maid. One Sunday the concert consisted of excerpts from the opera *William Tell*. Out of the silence came the barcarolle "Dark Forests" with the flutist alone, his solo rising in the summer air. The trees on Mt. Frugy leaned down to listen. The ones on the paths of Loc Maria offered themselves to the heavens. The flutist was spellbound: filled with emotion! That barcarolle was a declaration of love for the doctor's maid. She pressed the childish hands she was responsible for against her knees; she watched the bandstand in ecstasy. The nightingale's song! the lark's! the song of a love shared!

The circle of listeners broke up. The crowd drifted away.

Twenty years later I ran into the flutist: "I remember we left on maneuvers the same evening. By the time I got back to my garrison she'd left the village. I never spoke to her again."

Derniers poèmes (1945)

Conservatories

On the capstone of a well
a sundial's hand rests
marking the hour.
The hand wears a boxwood ring
What time is it? I'm frightened.
We have walked through tropical foliage
A ship enters the port
the princess returns from the hospital
The dark garden hides the pale fountain
We have walked through the greenery.
A flock of sheep returns from the palace.
On the capstone of the well
the hand is no longer alone
the shadow of a willow trembles on a sailboat in the
port.

Derniers poèmes

Burial in Quimper

No flowers you said no wreaths.
But April doesn't feel that way
they're a gift from the Lord
Look! You're already in Paradise.

April with its catafalques
of tulip poplars like algae
on innumerable bridges and under the branches
of chestnuts and hawthorns
buries your life that was like death
your virginal heroine's life.

I look through my tears.
Here death's neighbor is
that growth of dwarf palms:
Your hearse, my Delphine,
is one of those birds on the lawn.

When I was tired of tears
weary of journeys and grief
the foot of the Lord moved
in a patch of Parma violets.

Where will you come to, my heroine sister?
What jurisdiction
prouder than the loving nipple of the lilac
this April morning on the river bank
prouder than the violet seed of the rugged magnolia
its pistils hailing your little boat, o Valhalla!

With death, how soft your sofas feel to us
Spring so glorious on the banks of my river.

And the ancient store on your canal, cortege,
its old decaying balcony that tried to touch the earth
hiding me in summer while I read Maupassant.
I too bent, but from the vertical!

the courtyard! the studio! and the old tenants!
Past of my past, we are all passing through.
Past of my past, you alone are sorrowful.
Death is a spring that is not ephemeral.

Derniers poèmes

Our Earthly Virtues are Castles in the Air

You can tell you're dead when there's no more light: just broad daylight. I was living in a big white castle way up on the Butte Montmartre. When the king came, we'd put on a play and he'd appear on stage with the everyday elect to show there was no more glory, only greatness.

The lion and the wild boar fights held in the courtyard stood for my sins, the white dog fights the venial ones. The cemetery behind the castle was for the newly-dead and on the stairs I'd run into friends who were among the chosen. Two young enemies who'd done me lots of harm appeared beneath the terrace, looking up: "Ah, dead so young," I said. "What a pity for art!"

Derniers poèmes

In Paradise

Here I am in Paradise! Me, a feeble, rotting pumpkin? In Paradise? Impossible! Aren't there people you know? Who are knowing? Who are happy to be known? Everyone's got long hair from oiling it and the ones who were baldest on earth have the longest manes. I don't have any right to joke about such a holy place: but I just can't resist it! "It's me," says Pierre Colle, "Who are you? Pardon my mistake, but with your darkish halo I thought you were Miss Heylett (an operetta heroine from 1891) but you're too young to know that." "Hello, Gertrude": the scene is an art gallery. Gertrude's looking at me kindly. "O how handsome you are! Really! May I give you a kiss?" So we kissed. Then Gertrude stepped back: "Oh my. And who are you?"

"Max Jacob!" I repeated my name several times in a loud voice. Had she gone deaf? Deaf but kind.

Derniers poèmes

In the age of enchantment: "O those castles in the forest!" "I saw Dante's Beatrice. We are the same age. My earliest poems celebrate her hair, though I didn't have the nerve to read them to her."

In the age of feeling: "O the textbooks, the exams, the money worries!" "I saw my Beatrice on the stage. Women are sphinxes, I thought; they feed on a special kind of man passed through the bars of their cages."

In the age of grey hair—hers was dyed—I met my Beatrice at a cocktail party and with a smile told her of my youthful infatuation. "Oh, really," she answered, "That's odd." And I thought: "You old idiot."

Derniers poèmes

Christian Families

A great event took place at the religious school at
_____. An incredible miracle! A priest hit a
young man because he was making fun of him. The
adolescent swore that as Christ was his witness he had-
n't, and the marble Christ reached out and touched
the victim to bless him and with the same hand
slapped his abuser in the face. The whole class was on
its knees. Callings were born. And what do you think
happened? The families were up in arms. They took
their children out of the school not because a child
was hit, but because the education was "much too
mystical" (*sic*).

Derniers poèmes

If Guillaume's Death Had Been Christian

And I'd been so sure he was going to die that through my tears I'd drawn him on his deathbed. I must confess I even had formal concerns. Next day he was walking around Paris, strong and majestic. One morning at Sacré Coeur de Montmartre two big black cats squeezed me between them. A voice said, "Don't be afraid!" Sacré Coeur looked like one of those pink fortresses that adorn the summits of Italian hills, and he, Guillaume, high above, was like a bird with a man's head. Was he dead, our dear lyricist? My drawing wasn't finished. I bumped into him leading a group of disciples: was it he or Dante? Very much alive. Of course! Guillaume was not dead. A stout and clever priest said to me, "There's no one more alive than Guillaume Apollinaire. But finish your drawing of his death and put a silhouette of *me* on the lower left-hand side."

Derniers poèmes

At the outskirts of town where the forest of age-old trees begins, a man and a woman are standing naked. How grand they are! How gorgeous! The man asked the woman to sit at the base of an oak. She lay down and he mimed the action of pulling a blanket over their shoulders, but it wasn't a blanket . . . it was the whole suburb, the entire forest of age-old trees that buried them both.

Look! Up there in the loge! See those boxes? The lady with the long deer head and horns going all the way to the ceiling. Only it's not a deer's head, it's a skeleton. With the faces of wolves around it. The softly-dimming light gives a greenish cast to the show-case.

Derniers poèmes

Infernal Visions

The clear bright flames writhed around the zouave's britches. No one saw them, not even he. He was ordering: "A dozen oysters, to start. The cold partridge in aspic. After that, stuffed mushrooms. And what about a rum soufflé before the fruit?" Under the table were shapely naked women. The flames climbed with voluptuous claws. Somewhere an angel wept. "Can't you see the fire?" a child asked.

Derniers poèmes

The Pilgrims at Emmaeus

I don't know who was there: it was one of those bistros where my youth vanished. A white marble table in the corner and the usual mirror that ran the length of the wall, turned and continued. I was wearing a ratty bowler and a look that questioned the sickly cast in the eye of the Lord. (Even though he looked more like John the Baptist it was really him!) "Since you're God and you know everything, tell me when this war will be over and," I added, "who will win." "You want me to tell you so you can become a barroom prophet?" He was silent. Night fell. There were no drinks on the table.

Derniers poèmes

Write Your Memoirs

Who remembers Passy before the Eiffel Tower? All the witnesses are dead, except maybe for me. From a bateau-mouche you could see in the distance a city of white houses and big buildings. That's where Rosa-Josepha, the circus phenomenon (no one used the term music-hall yet) lived in a first-floor apartment. She was a doll with two sets of limbs in brown velour playing on a rug. A dark woman in white lace paid no attention to her. In the courtyard of the apartment building I saw in a tilbury a Moldavian officer in dress uniform whose opulence her managers were paying for. A brother? A husband? The memory of that visit hasn't remained. I had to go back to the Place de la Republique by tram but I stayed on longer, as far as Vincennes. Along the way I lost a little old suitcase. A man in grey was waiting under a chestnut tree. It was me. Rosa-Josepha has two souls in a single body while I have one soul in two.

Derniers poèmes

Novel 1943

On horseback! that's how we left: by God, I handled myself well enough. Are you surprised? Not as much as I was. The palace in the desert is covered with carvings and inscriptions that occupied me less than my mount did. I said to myself: who knows if in twenty centuries the Arc de Triomphe on the Place d'Etoile will be the destination of tourist trips in a desert and if I myself . . . But I don't believe in metempsychosis, so what am I going to say about it? Being a guide would suit me if it weren't for all the coming and going and caring for horses. A guy with a detachable collar and a monocle helps me with that: "During the time I was a journalist in Paris . . ." He speaks enthusiastically of the café crèmes of Les Halles. My rosy cheeks and full shoulders got me out of trouble one more time and out of Transatlantic Steamship and here I am a millionaire again in a capital city staying with an American, getting fat and round under the exquisite wool of my jacket; it's a time for collecting curios and writing my memoirs. It doesn't matter that I'm bankrupt: let's make a deal.

Derniers poèmes

Magic Confession

"You never take me on your trips anymore." "Look!" "I see a dark desert divided symmetrically by an endless number of walls. But where are the roads?" "On top of the walls." Dark, isolated roads: we're in China.

The blind horse put at my disposal for our trips was formerly a worker who had broken both legs and made a futile attempt to become a roofer. He spent his time watching houses being built. Then he went blind and later became a horse. When I was working at Pohu's farm he got attached to me and when my bicycle was stolen during the harvest of 1900, he suggested I travel with him. That's how we got to Ville-Miroir where my love story took place. I think I can sum it up in a sentence or two: a woman I met at carnival time was changed into a library and when, to possess her, I learned every book in the Bagario Palace by heart, she became a woman again. And what a woman! She wanted to be a big movie star. I spent every cent my good name was worth on treats, dinners, bribes, outfits, pocket money. Come on, here, take it. Yes, I leaped willingly into the secret night of jealousy. She left on my blind horse who brought her back to me worn out, indifferent, deceived, abused. It goes without saying we forgave each other completely.

"Let's go live in your home town," she said. There were three of us on the blind horse: the third was me as a farm hand.

When we got to Pohu's farm there was nothing

but a big sign with these words on it: *Sightseeing by Plane*. "Such competition," the blind horse said sadly, lying down on the grass. We had to prod him to get him going again.

Derniers poèmes

The Seasons

Spring is the cradle of love.

At Balmoral Castle, on a footbridge across the river Dee, I saw Spanish grandees drunk with spring. I think the Dalai Lama is sensitive to its green shoots. As for me, I'm searching for God in wintertime.

Down with the picrocholes, say the bears in their summer velvet. Is it really possible the southern hemisphere has summer while we're freezing? Victorious miserable sun, turning the wise men of Toulouse into singers. So much for orthodoxy! And this the hallmark of your law: everything flesh is sunlight condensed. It's not for nothing that pears are shaped like the cheeks of adolescents. Sunlight! Trucks from celestial factories. As for me, I only see summer through telescope or microscope. I've lost everything. I'm searching for God in winter.

Let's go where the snow is! into that noble darkness at the spinning poles.

"As long as you don't leave your room."

"Just let me raise the curtain."

"If you move your chair you're risking a head-cold."

Let me see that gorgeous young woman again. When I raise the curtain I see her and I'm magnetized and mesmerized. Her bare feet in the snow like King

Henry at Canossa. A wreath of wheat stalks sparkling on her blond hair. With the fingers of a milliner setting a hat just right, she forms a crown of thorns shaped to fit my skull:

"For you!"

Derniers poèmes

"Max is a Lunatic" (Everyone)

Let's consider . . . let's consider the number of inhabited worlds. Despite this spring evening with its wild grasses (aha! they too!), daisies and buttercups knee-high, I sense fear in you caused by the Great Universal Conch: should I, as everyone says, should I be called a lunatic? Let's consider it! God makes madmen of those he would destroy. Whereas God in his goodness cannot but wish to save me: therefore I am not mad. But if I were, hasn't God said:

"You who are insane, come to me."

My God, as one who is insane, I come to you and not to the devil the way other lunatics do. And if I go to you it's clear I'm not a lunatic. Q.E.D.

The majority of my reflections concern purely natural phenomena like the swarms of gold midges which are simply madmen's hallucinations and exist only as indications that other midges, not golden, exist, because nature abhors a vacuum. Most definitely! Abhors a vacuum. You who can see see those electrons, those ions and the entire ultra-violet of the warm blood cells. You who can hear hear the intervals and overtones of the kilometric silence of the heavens. Abhors a vacuum! It's a matter of knowing how to hear the rustling of the Great Kilometric Shell. A tree like a waiter in a café loaded down with saucers of poison. I'm discussing the elderflower that sends out narcotic ribbons called in another language "fireworks" . . . but who knows the language the angels use? Those narcotic ribbons are my shroud. The shroud of little bald menhirs in motion like myself. Nevertheless, they're nothing like the hallucinations of madness and science that goes by the name of physical chemistry (and not psychiatry) which will soon explain how many electrons it takes to make a shroud or what the language of flowers is or (known anyhow) the language of angels. Elderflower alphabet, I don't abhor a vacuum, but I am afraid of the ethereal hell called the void and the Great Kilometric Cockleshell.

O pardon me! I very nearly . . . just pay attention, madame. With the tip of my menhir toe, I very nearly . . . Greetings, greetings, madame (watch out: handle those envoys from ethereal hells with care). Greetings, Madame Mandrake (everyone knows what a mandrake is: let me graciously offer it a sweet). You've been exposed, Madame Mandrake. I nearly booted you into the Loire: what's it like to have a head no bigger than a waxed hazelnut. It's not your yellow ant panache or your frogs' legs that will save you from being crushed. Not everyone has my tact! You have something to say to me? Oh, pardon me! I thought with your reproachful attitude you were going to start that eternal defense of the devil's envoys. Speak, you go ahead! Speak, madame, speak. Speak, you have my permission, though with a flick of my foot I can send you into the Loire. (Let's be careful!) Speak! I'm listening. Wait, let me tip my beret, I'm saluting you (hypocrite). The eternal defense of satanic things, to know No. 1 that I belong to hell and not heaven; No. 2 that the number of my connivings and my outrages . . . yes! okay, enough! No! I won't allow it. I know myself better than the devil and you don't know me. So then, madmen don't weep with remorse, Madame, they

laugh! they laugh! they laugh! they laugh! . . . they . . .
laugh! But let's reason together, since you, too, seem
reasonable: if I were what they call "mad," a madman,
a real one, I wouldn't know the language of the trees,
or reveal the true personality of roots, or wait patiently
before a mandrake . . . patiently.

I think it's time to go lie down. Most of what
we call insane is just stupid.

Derniers poèmes

Loving Thy Neighbor

Who's watched a toad cross the street? He looks like a very small man: no bigger than a doll. He crawls along on his knees: do we say he looks ashamed? . . . no! That he's got rheumatism. A leg drags behind, he pulls it forward. Where's he headed like this? He came up out of the sewer, poor clown. No one noticed him on the street. Long time ago no one noticed me. Now the children mock my yellow star. Lucky toad, you don't have a yellow star.

Derniers poèmes

The Yellow Star Again

"**A**re those beets your dog's eating?"
"No, it's a Jew who fell down in the snow."
"They could find some other place to faint instead of my sidewalk."

Derniers poèmes

Death

The body cold and stiff in the morgue of the world who will give its life back so it may leave?

The morgue mountain is on my body who will free its life so it may leave?

Eyes advance like a cloud of bees the eyes of Argus or the lamb of the Apocalypse.

The cloud has thawed my body's morgue. A place, understand me, for the sweet coming of the Lord.

Finally, the body's little more than a faint outline the eyes of the cloud gone too.

What's left barely the size of a steak: a bloodstain, some bits of marble in memory of a lost name.

Derniers poèmes

Ballad of the Perpetual Miracle

That God exists is incredible
and this journey to us, starting 2000 years ago
incredible
that animals and plants live
that God doesn't die, incredible
and the empty cage
the bones become.
I stop here because
I cannot elevate my soul. No, I cannot . . . incredible
a moment of emptiness and God returning.
Call it agony if you will or the void, critical
change, death—incredible—
Astonishing life! monstrous denial of God
even as my spirit, my own void calls him "God! God
    alone!"
incredible.
I call the genies of the four corners of the earth
Help me, priest-magicians.
I call the nebulous white snake, magician I.
The giant comes who has had nine mothers
making three attempts to chain the wolf to the beaches
    of earth.
Amazing that God might have a forehead, a mouth, a
    cave, a mother!
There are seven caves and four bouquets
the nebulous white snake
and four live geese to celebrate my madness
incredible
that God exists, incredible!

Derniers poèmes

The Restless Soul Remakes Heaven

I saw the Lord at the bottom of a river. The water was transparent. His robe was dark but not soiled or wet. A dark shell in my hands, a pearl inside it . . . symbol of what? Sleeping naiad, are you the image of my soul? My lazy soul that naiad! When he awoke the Lord's robe was covered with arabesques. He rolled side to side like a swimmer and His Face deigned to meet mine on the shore. So you came back to life, heavenly nature, just as my soul leaped up. The calm succession of waves beneath the trees of Paradise boiled on the sand. The shell glowed softly in my hand as I watched the pearls turn ruby-red.

Derniers poèmes

Prophetic Dreams

I dreamed of a beautiful lake
and the reflection of dark cliffs.
Next day I found my emerald.
I dreamed of a beautiful road and the ring of iron
   hooves.
But I was stopped at its edge by a wall
of red rocks that vanished in sky and sea.
I dreamed of an exquisite meal where I was served
   roast pork.
But all I saw was my hostess shining like a Christian
   Olympus.
I dreamed of the altar and the Mass
a parapet
Benares
and the Hindu paradise.
I dreamed of you from one room to the next
my immaculate youth.
And I dreamed of an old man torn to shreds
by the white phantom of time.

Derniers poèmes

Artless Lines

For a long time I thought of life as an autumn fog
of distant lakes cleaved by yellow sand,
of dry branch and dull bush.
And then, once, at a hunting lodge,
I met a bird wearing a crown
Who said "Speak to me. Ask me who I am."
A voice answered "Love! Safe conduct!"
The path of my fate is, I'm afraid, unwavering.
I'll soon be at death's door.
I'll leave gladly what others have envied me for,
an adolescent's heart treasured like a precious urn.
Life is a square dance your hand in the one nearest
    yours.
Swift is the race hard the rocky place
and the flower of love died beneath our knees
while the lips cried silently in the depths of the heart.
An angel of the Lord came to me:
"Use your voice to sing to heaven!"
It was a wise spirit and beautiful too.
And since then! How often has God whispered:
"Silence is everywhere but in my eyes.
Become intoxicated with me. Look for me more and
    more.
Contemplate me: I promise nothing.
And think carefully: my image is in you.
Your secret happiness in the midst of sorrow.
Understand my law of suffering

transform your grief into holy ecstasy
through my eyes you must see your nature
through my heart you must weep with love."

Derniers poèmes

Reconstruction

All it takes is a five-year-old in pale blue overalls drawing in a coloring book for a door to open into the light, for the house to be built again and the ochre hillside covered with flowers.

Derniers poèmes

Acknowledgments

The American Poetry Review: "1914," "1889-1916," "The Key," "The Feminist Question," "Poem," "A Bit of Art Criticism," "Achilles' Wheel," "Hell Has Gradations," "Jean Jacques," "Ballad of the Night Visitor," "If Guillaume's Death Had Been Christian," "Christian Families," "Infernal Visions," "Burial in Quimper," "Reconstruction."

Denver Quarterly: "Foreword to *The Dice Cup*," "Memoirs of a Spy," "Searching for the Traitor," "Watered Earth."

Some of these poems appeared, slightly modified, in *Twenty-Three Poems from Max Jacob* (The Cummington Press, 1994), revisions by Harry Duncan.

Although this project was aided by a Translation Fellowship from the National Endowment for the Arts, it would not have reached its present form without the insight and enthusiasm of my dear friend and colleague, Lucy Aghazarian, whose vast knowledge of the resources of both French and English was of immeasurable help in re-creating the voice of Max Jacob.